Copyright © 2022 Arro

Published by Arrowto

Huntly
New Zealand 3700

info@arrowtownpress.com

All rights reserved. Reproduction in whole or in part without written permission of the publisher is strictly prohibited.

Check out our range of children's books at arrowtownpress.com.

Table of Contents

Introduction	1
What is a Cave?	4
Types of Caves	6
Limestone caves	6
Lava caves	7
Ice caves	8
Great Caves	9
Mammoth Cave	10
Krubera Cave	15
The Waitomo Glowworm Cave	19
The Eisriesenwelt Ice Cave	23
The Cave of the Crystals	26
Black Water Rafting	28
Cave Diving	31
Cave Animals and Plants	32
Ra Paulette	37
The Last Word	39

Introduction

Deep beneath the earth's surface, hidden from the sunlight, lies a world of mystery and wonder. Caves are ancient natural wonders that have fascinated people from the beginning of time. Imagine winding through dark passages, discovering hidden underground rivers and lakes, and seeing sparkling crystals and colorful rock formations. From the longest caves to the deepest caves, from the most colorful caves to the most unique caves, there is so much to explore and discover. Are you ready to embark on an exciting journey to discover the greatest caves in the world? Pack your bags, grab your flashlight, and let's go!

We'll start by exploring the longest cave in the world, Mammoth Cave. This cave is over 400 miles long and it's so big that if you were to walk all its passages, it would take you months! You'll be amazed by the different levels and chambers that this cave has to offer.

Next, we'll venture to the deepest cave in the world, Krubera Cave. This cave is over 7,200 feet deep and it is home to some of the rarest and most unique animals on earth. You'll be amazed by the underground rivers and lakes that you'll discover in this cave.

Climbing in one of the Waitomo caves.

Then, we'll visit the most mystical cave in the world, Waitomo Glowworm Cave. This cave system is filled with millions of tiny glowing worms that light up like stars in the sky. You'll feel like you're in a magical underground world as you float silently through the worm-lit cave in a boat.

Next, we'll explore one of the most unique caves in the world, Eisriesenwelt Ice Cave. This cave is made of ice and rock and it's like nothing you've ever seen before. It's a winter wonderland underground, with icicles, frozen waterfalls and more.

This is perhaps the oldest cave painting ever discovered. It comes from the Leang Tedongnge cave in a remote valley on the island of Sulawesi, Indonesia. Experts believe it to be 45000 years old.

Finally, we'll travel to Mexico to visit the Cave of the Crystals. This cave is hot, humid and the home of the most beautiful and large crystals imaginable.

Caves are not just holes in the ground. They are underground worlds of natural beauty and wonder. Join us on this adventure and discover the secrets of caves!

CAVE FACT Experts say that we've only discovered about 1% of all the caves on Earth.

WHAT IS A CAVE?

Caves are natural underground openings in the earth. They are formed by the erosion of rock over millions of years by water, wind, and other natural forces.

The unique environments found in caves are home to many unusual plants and animals. Caves are dark and they keep a constant cool temperature year-round. The plants and animals that live in them have adapted to survive in these conditions. For example, some cave animals, like bats, have evolved to use echolocation, which allows them to navigate and find food in the dark. Echolocation is the process of bouncing their squeaks off solid surfaces. The bat's brain then works out exactly where it is from these echoes. Echolocation is the biological form of electronic sonar!

Reed Flute cave China. The Chinese people also know this cave as "the Palace of Natural Art."

Many caves have unique rock formations that are created over thousands of years by water dripping through cracks and holes in the rock. These formations are called stalactites and stalagmites. Stalactites are prongs of stone that grow like teeth from the top of the cave. Stalagmites are stone teeth that grow up from the floor of the cave. Caves frequently have underground lakes and rivers, which add to their unique and thrilling environments. These underground lakes are homes to strange and unusual aquatic life.

Scientists value caves because they provide information about Earth's history. Scientists can study the layers of rock in a cave to learn about historic climate patterns and the types of plants and animals that once lived in the area. Caves are also extremely important for learning about human history. Cave paintings provide information about how our ancestors lived 45,000 years ago. Ancient tools and other artifacts are also found in caves.

And then there is cave diving and black water rafting. These are extreme sports people do in caves that are either full of water or have rivers running through them. There is also an artist in America who, by himself, digs caves and turns them into some of the most beautiful artworks in the world.

Read on to learn more about cave sports, cave animals and cave artists!

This is a beach inside the entrance to the gigantic Hang Son Doong cave. A shaft of sunlight lights the beach which is deep inside the cave!

Types of Caves

Caves come in many different forms and are created by a variety of natural processes. Some of the most common types of caves include limestone caves, lava caves, and ice caves.

CAVE FACT Most caves don't have an entrance which is why most caves are still undiscovered.

Limestone Caves

Water erosion of limestone rock creates limestone caves. Limestone is a soft type of rock that is made when minerals in water settle in layers over enormous periods of time. These minerals come from dissolved shells and similar marine life. Because limestone is a soft stone, rain and rivers gouge out underground caverns and passages over time. Some famous limestone caves include the Carlsbad Caverns in New Mexico and Mammoth Cave in Kentucky. Waitomo in New Zealand has some of the most beautiful and unique limestone caves in the world.

Limestone caves frequently have lakes, rivers, and amazing rock formations.

LAVA CAVES

Lava caves are formed when molten rock, called lava, flows down a volcano's slopes and the outside layer of the flow cools and solidifies. The lava inside continues to flow leaving behind a hollow tube of hard lava. Lava caves can be found on many volcanoes around the world. The Thurston Lava Tube in Hawaii is one of the most famous. Called 'Nāhuku' or 'the protuberances' in Hawaiian, it can be visited and explored in the National Park on the Big Island of Hawai'i.

Thurston Lava Tube in Hawaii.

ICE CAVES

Ice Caves are formed by the deposit and erosion of glacial ice. This process creates underground passageways and caverns that feature amazing ice structures. The Blue Ice Cave in Iceland and the Eisriesenwelt Ice Cave in Austria are two of the most famous ice caves. Ice caves are often formed around limestone and lava tube caves. If it is cold and there is plenty of snow and ice in the mix, you can make the claim that you are in an ice cave!

Eisriesenwelt Ice Cave.

An ice cave in Iceland's Langjökull glacier.

 **CAVE FACT** Cavers are very meticulous about their headlamps. There is no light inside deep caves. This means you must bring a good headlamp and plenty of spares. Cavers usually carry three individual light sources.

Great Caves

There are many great caves dotted all around the world. There may be caves near to you ... or even under you! Remember, never go into a cave without an adult who is knowledgeable about the cave in question. Caves might be fascinating but they can also be very dangerous! Anyway, we're going to look at five amazing caves from the four corners of our world.

 **CAVE FACT** The Tennessee, Alabama, and Georgia area of the United States contains about 14,000 known caves. This area used to be a shallow sea which resulted in plenty of limestone - an ideal material for the creation of caves.

Mammoth Cave provides a wonderful adventure for all ages.
In this photo we see a fog bank that sometimes develops inside Mammoth Cave.

Mammoth Cave

Mammoth Cave is the longest cave in the world. It is in the state of Kentucky in the United States. Mammoth Cave was formed by the erosion of limestone over millions of years. The Green River is one of many that flow through the Mammoth Cave network and cause the erosion.

A lake in Mammoth Cave.

Mammoth is made up of more than 400 miles of passageways. To give you an idea of what 400 miles in a straight line looks like, think about this: Los Angeles in California and Scottsdale in Arizona are about 400 miles apart!

CAVE FACT Humans have used caves for shelter throughout history. Recently, cave divers discovered some magnificent underwater caves in Yucatan that were used by the Aztecs as temples about 500 years ago.

Mammoth Cave has its own unique ecosystem. Several species of bats, crickets, and fish have adapted to live in the dark and cold conditions of this cave system. These creatures are only found in Mammoth Cave. Scientists have also found evidence of ancient human habitation within the cave dating back around 10,000 years!

CAVE FACT Even world-renowned cave experts will speak to local experts before entering a cave. Local expertise is essential to understanding the risks and dangers of a cave system.

Visitors to Mammoth Cave can take guided tours to explore the cave and learn more about its history and geology. The park offers different types of tours, from easy scenic tours for the whole family to intense and challenging tours for experienced cavers. Some areas of Mammoth Cave are closed to the public to protect its fragile ecosystems. Mammoth Cave is also a National Park and a UNESCO World Heritage Site, which means it's protected and preserved for future generations to enjoy.

Mammoth Cave has a rich history that dates back thousands of years. European settlers first discovered the cave in the early 1800s, but it is believed that local indigenous peoples and early settlers knew of the cave's existence well before the 1800s.

John Houchin made the first recorded discovery of the cave we know of in 1797. He stumbled upon the cave while hunting.

CAVE FACT Cave exploring is known as "spelunking." A cave explorer is a "spelunker." A cave researcher is a "speleologist."

This stone shack is the remains of an experiment held in Mammoth Cave over 170 years ago. In 1842 about 12 tuberculosis patients were housed in the cave because it was thought the cool, pure cave air might help them to recover.

The cave's true significance was not fully realized until the 1820s when Stephen Bishop began giving guided tours of the cave. Bishop was a slave who worked on the land where the cave is located, and he became an expert cave guide. He explored the cave extensively and discovered many of the passages and features that visitors see today. In the following years, the cave became a popular tourist destination, and it was also studied by scientists who were interested in its geology and history. As the years passed, more and more of the cave was explored and mapped, and it was discovered that the cave system was much larger than originally thought.

CAVE FACT The largest known cave by volume is the Hang Son Doong in Vietnam, at 600 feet high, 300 feet wide, and 3 miles long!

Mammoth Cave is a unique and fascinating place with many interesting facts and figures. Here are just a few examples:

- The cave is so large that it has its own unique ecosystem, which includes several species of bats, crickets, and fish that have adapted to live in the dark and cold conditions of the cave.
- The cave has an average temperature of 54 degrees Fahrenheit all year round.
- The cave has several underground rivers, including the Echo River, which visitors can take boat rides on during some tours.
- The cave has many different types of rock formations, such as stalactites and stalagmites, that have been created by dripping water over vast periods of time.
- The cave is also home to several historic sites, such as the "Old Guide's Cemetery," which is the final resting place of some of the early explorers and guides of the cave.
- In 1981, Mammoth Cave was declared a UNESCO World Heritage Site, which means it's protected and preserved for future generations to enjoy.
- Mammoth Cave is nearly twice as long as the second longest cave system we know of; Mexico's Sac Actun underwater cave.

 **CAVE FACT** Caves can be dangerous, mostly because they're prone to flooding. It takes extended and heavy rain to flood most caves.

Krubera Cave

Krubera Cave is a limestone cave located in the Western Caucasus Mountains of Abkhazia, Georgia. Krubera Cave is famous as the deepest known cave in the world, with a depth of 7,208 feet.

Speleologists gradually explored and mapped Krubera over many years. These explorers and scientists reached the current depth measurement of 7,208 feet in 2012.

The cave is known for its challenging and dangerous conditions, with narrow passages and treacherous underground rivers. The cave is also home to several unique species of fauna, such as the cave beetle and the cavefish.

A deep shaft in the Krubera cave.

The shaft viewed from the other end.

The various expeditions of the cave have found many different levels, each with its own unique features and challenges. The cave is also home to the deepest underwater sump, a point where the cave becomes flooded and only experienced divers can go further.

Like Mammoth Cave, Krubera was formed by the erosion of limestone by underground rivers. This process created a vast and complex system of passageways, caverns, and underground lakes. One of the most striking features of the cave is the variety of cave formations, such as stalactites, stalagmites, flowstones, and rimstone dams. The cave also has an underground lake called "The Bottomless Pit".

 **CAVE FACT** Most caves are limestone caves. This is because limestone dissolves easily in rainwater. Limestone is made from sea organisms, like coral, shells, and clams.

Krubera Cave was first explored in 1960 by a group of Soviet speleologists. The cave's depth was gradually explored and mapped by speleologists from various countries over the years. Here are some more facts about the cave:

- The Krubera Cave is the deepest known cave in the world. It has a depth of over 7,200 feet.
- Krubera Cave is one of five caves in the Arabika Massif mountain block to reach depths of more than 3,000 feet.
- The cave was named after the Russian geographer Alexander Kruber, who explored it in the early 20th century.
- It is home to several species of bats, as well as various species of arthropods, such as spiders and

centipedes, that have adapted to life in complete darkness.

- The exploration of the cave is challenging and requires specialized caving techniques and equipment, as well as physical fitness and endurance. Despite this, it remains a popular destination for experienced cavers from around the world.

- The deepest living terrestrial animal found on earth can be found in Krubera Cave. This is a 0.12-inch springtail with no eyes and is believed to survive on fungus and organic material. It can live as far as 6,000 feet deep into the earth. A springtail is a six-legged creepy crawly that looks like an insect but isn't. They are found all over the world and are known to be great jumpers.

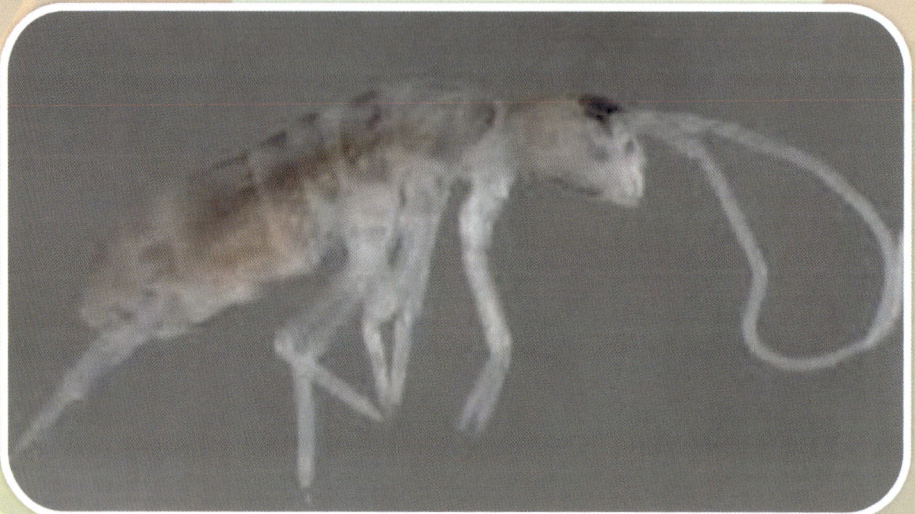

The Krubera Cave springtail.

Hang Son Doong cave.

CAVE FACT One cubic inch of stalagmite or stalactite takes about 1,000 years to form.

The Waitomo Glowworm Cave

The Waitomo Glowworm Cave is a limestone cave located in the Waikato region of New Zealand. The cave is famous for its glowworms. Glowworms are small insects that emit a very bright blue-green light. The glowworms and their amazing lights create a unique and beautiful underground effect. They make an underground galaxy of stars. There are many stunning caves around the world but the Waitomo glowworm cave can rightfully claim to be one of the most beautiful of them all.

These are glowworms. The very bottom of the thread glows. They are technically not worms. The picture shows the larvae of a gnat but "glowworm" sounds better than "glowgnatlarvae."

An English surveyor named Fred Mace and Maori Chief Tane Tinorau discovered the cave in 1887. The two men were exploring the area and stumbled upon the cave's entrance. The display of thousands of glowworms amazed them, and they quickly realized the cave's potential as a tourist attraction.

The cave is a popular tourist destination, and visitors can take guided tours of the cave, where they can see the glowworms up close and experience the cave's unique beauty. The tours typically include a boat ride through the cave's underground river, which provides a great view of the glowworms.

This is the boat ride in the famous glowworm cave.

Entering Ruakuri cave - another of the amazing caves you can explore in Waitomo.

Stalactites are shards of rock that grow down from the roof of a cave.

Here are some more interesting facts about the Waitomo Glowworm Cave:

- The glowworms in the cave are the larvae of a species of fly called Arachnocampa Luminosa.
- The glowworms produce a blue-green light through a chemical reaction in their bodies.
- The light produced by the glowworms is used to attract prey, such as small insects.
- The cave has many different chambers, each with its own unique features and formations.
- The cave is also home to several species of bats.
- The cave is a protected area, and the number of visitors is limited to protect the environment and the glowworms.

- The Vienna Boys' Choir, among others, has performed in the largest part of the cave which is known as the Cathedral.

Another huge cavern in a limestone cave.

 **CAVE FACT** Hundreds of millions of years ago a sea called the North American Inland Sea covered much of North America. This sea created lots of limestone and limestone means caves. Kentucky is believed to have the most caves of any US State.

Eisriesenwelt Ice Cave

The Eisriesenwelt Ice Cave, located in Werfen, Austria, is one of the most unique and spectacular caves in the world. This amazing cave is a natural limestone cave - with extras. The Austrian Alps provide this cave with unique and spectacular ice formations. The combination of river erosion and the mountain glaciers created this truly breathtaking natural wonder.

The cave is more than 26 miles long, making it the largest ice cave in the world. Visitors can explore the cave on a guided tour, which takes them through a series of chambers and corridors filled with ice sculptures, frozen waterfalls, and crystal-clear ice formations. The cave is constantly changing and evolving, with new ice wonders forming every winter and melting every summer.

Eisriesenwelt ice cave.

Anton Posselt, a German speleologist discovered the Eisriesenwelt Ice Cave in 1879. Some people claim that locals knew of the cave before this but believed it was a place inhabited by bad spirits and kept away.

Organized tours began in 1912 and Eisriesenwelt ice cave has been open to the public ever since.

Improvements over the years include new paths and stairways built for ease of access. Today, the cave is a popular tourist destination, and visitors from all over the world come to see the unique beauty of the cave and the ice formations.

Eisriesenwelt ice cave.

Interesting facts and figures about the cave:

- The Eisriesenwelt Ice Cave is the largest ice cave in the world, with a total length of about 26 miles.
- The cave is unique in that it is the only ice cave in the world that is open to the public.
- The cave's temperature stays at a constant 32.9 °F.

- The Eisriesenwelt caves are situated in Werfen, a small idyllic village approximately 40km south of Salzburg.

- The cave is home to several species of bats.

- Thousands of tourists visit the cave every year, making it one of the most popular tourist attractions in Austria.

- The cave offers a range of different experiences, from guided walking tours to ice climbing.

- The cave is also home to a natural history museum, which offers visitors the chance to learn about the geology and history of the cave and the surrounding area.

The Cave of the Crystals

The Cave of the Crystals is a natural marvel located in Chihuahua, Mexico. It is a unique geological formation that contains some of the largest natural crystals ever discovered. Some of these crystals measure 40 feet in length! These giant selenite crystals formed over millions of years from a combination of factors, including the unique mineral-rich water that flows through the cave, the high temperatures, and the absence of light. Visitors to the cave are struck by the sheer size and beauty of the crystals, which glimmer and reflect light in a mesmerizing display.

The Cave of the Crystals in Mexico.

Despite its breath-taking beauty, the Cave of the Crystals is a dangerous place, as the high humidity and temperatures can be harmful to visitors. As a result, access to the cave is strictly controlled and visitors are only allowed to view the crystals from a safe distance. Despite these limitations, the Cave of the Crystals remains a popular destination for tourists and scientists alike, who are drawn to its unique and awe-inspiring natural beauty. Some interesting facts about the Cave of the Crystals include:

- The Cave of Crystals is located in Chihuahua, Mexico and is part of the Naica Mine complex.
- The giant crystals in the Cave of Crystals are estimated to be around 500,000 years old.

- The giant selenite crystals in the cave formed due to a unique combination of mineral-rich water, high temperatures, and the lack of light.
- Some bacteria living in the cave do not match any other known life forms on planet Earth.
- Access to the Cave of Crystals is strictly controlled due to the high humidity and temperatures of over 120 degrees Fahrenheit.

It is over 120 degrees Fahrenheit in the Cave of the Crystals!

 **CAVE FACT** Some caves are created by tides. These caves flood like clockwork with the incoming tide. This never-ending process creates the caverns.

Black Water Rafting

Have you heard of white-water rafting? Adventurers in inflatable rafts thunder down the whitewater or rapid sections of powerful rivers. Black water rafting is very different to this. Black water rafting occurs when people ride the rivers that flow through enormous caves.

Black water rafters drift under a million glowworms in one of the many caves at Waitomo.

Instead of large rafts, each cave rafter has their own car tire inner tube for this exciting adventure. Once you reach the river portion of the cave you jump into the water and sit on the inner tube as you drift through the cave. It is called black water rafting because the water in caves looks black and the overall environment is dark and mysterious.

 **CAVE FACT** It's a tradition that the person who discovers the cave gets to name it. Not every country or state allows this, but most U.S. states allow you to name it if you are the first person to find the cave.

Cave enthusiasts in New Zealand's beautiful Waitomo area came up with black water rafting. Many everyday cave visitors saw these early black water rafters and asked if they could go with them. Very soon black water rafting became a very successful business in Waitomo.

Waitomo is famous for its beautiful glowworm cave. There are, however, many explorable caves in the region and some of the black water rafting caves have great glowworm displays too.

Another photo of black water rafters in a Waitomo cave.

On one of the Waitomo black water rafting routes, you get to jump off the top of an underground waterfall! It is off-the-scale thrilling.

Not only do have your own inner tube but you also wear a thick wetsuit to keep warm. On your head you wear a caving helmet with a light. Black water rafting is a family adventure and anyone who is reasonably fit and healthy and has a passion for exploration can go on an underground black water rafting river journey.

Cave Diving

Cave diving is an exciting and challenging adventure that takes daredevils deep into the world of flooded caves. This type of diving is different from other types of diving because it takes the dangers of deep-sea diving and adds the extra difficulties of the enclosed nature of caves. This means that if something goes badly wrong there is usually no easy way to launch a rescue. Poor visibility, tearing currents and confined spaces are some of the many risks faced by cave divers. Only very experienced divers can dive deep into caves. It is so dangerous that even extremely experienced divers can get into trouble inside caves.

Cave divers.

Despite the danger, experienced divers are drawn to the thrill and excitement of cave diving. It may take only an hour or so to reach the deepest part of a cave but it can take literally days to return to the cave's entrance. Cave divers, like deep ocean divers, must decompress for many hours on the way to the surface.

Cave divers have to be careful not to disturb the settled silt and sand. If they do, then this beautiful clear water can become so cloudy that there is no visibility at all.

CAVE FACT Geologists think that there are many undiscovered caves that contain caverns that are large enough to fit entire cities.

Cave Animals and Plants

A cave salamander. It has little color and is blind.

Caves provide isolated environments that can harbor a range of unusual animals and plants. Due to the lack of light, many species found in caves have adapted heightened senses to compensate for their lack of sight. Some examples of strange animals found in caves include:

- Cave crickets - these large, flightless insects have elongated hind legs and a tendency to make chirping noises.
- Some New Zealand caves have the fearsome giant weta. Some species of weta can catch birds!
- Cavefish - some species of fish living in caves have lost the ability to see, while others have developed an increased sense of touch or hearing
- Cave salamanders - these amphibians have adapted to life in total darkness by losing pigmentation and having very well-developed hearing and sense of touch.
- Blind beetles - many species of beetles that live in caves have adapted to life without light by developing heightened senses of touch and smell
- Cave spiders - these arachnids have often developed the ability to spin webs without the use of visual cues.

This is a weta. They only live in New Zealand - and they can be quite large. Imagine finding one of these guys in the toe of your gumboot as you were getting ready to explore a cave. It happens!

In case you were wondering, these are gumboots. They are high fashion in New Zealand. New Zealanders make sculptures of gumboots and sing songs about them! They are required kit for a casual caver.

This is a traditional New Zealand sculpture of a gumboot.

Bats love caves.

This is cave fungus.

As for plants and mushrooms, there are a few species that grow in caves, such as:

- Cave fungi - these fungi have adapted to life in the dark by producing their own light through bioluminescence
- Cave moss - some species of moss have evolved to be able to photosynthesize in the low light levels found in caves
- Cave ferns - these ferns have adapted to life in caves by developing the ability to survive in low light levels.

Glowworms are not the only glowing lifeforms. Some cave mushrooms glow too.

Ra Paulette

Ra Paulette is an inspirational artist. He digs and sculpts large caves by hand all by himself in New Mexico, USA. Paulette's work is characterized by his use of natural light and his intricate, organic designs that evoke the natural beauty of the rock he works with and the underground spaces he creates.

This is part of a cave Ra Paulette dug and sculptured by hand.

Paulette excavates sandstone cliffs by hand, using only basic tools and his own physical strength. The result is a series of stunning, awe-inspiring spaces that invite the viewer to explore the beauty of nature and the power of the human imagination.

Art critics recognize Paulette's work for its creativity, technical mastery, and environmental sensitivity. Numerous documentaries have explored his life and art. In addition to his sculptures, Paulette is also a writer and a passionate advocate for environmental conservation, using his art to raise awareness about the importance of preserving our planet's natural wonders.

Ra Paulette brings new meaning to the term 'cave art.'

Despite his success, Paulette remains a humble and dedicated artist, driven by a passion for his craft and a deep love of nature. His work serves as a testament to the power of the human spirit, and an inspiration to all who appreciate majestic art.

THE LAST WORD

Hi there, thanks for looking at my book on caves. I live about an hour's drive from Waitomo. My favorite adventure when I was very young was to visit the Glowworm cave. As an adult, I have gone black water rafting several times. It is affordable and very exciting. If you ever make it to New Zealand, I cannot recommend Waitomo and all its wonders enough!

All the best

Lucy

More Books by Lucy

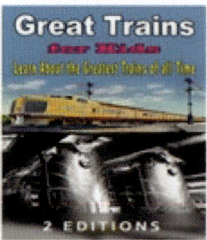   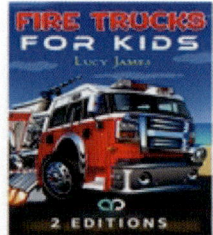

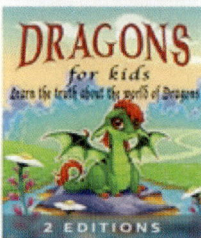   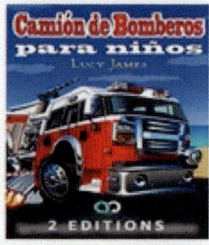

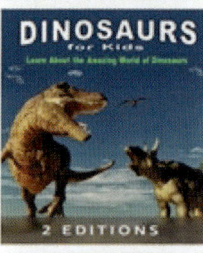 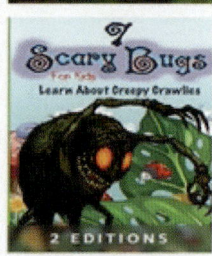  

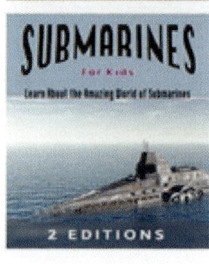 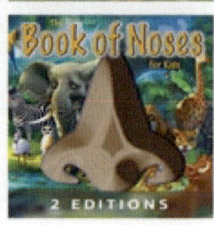 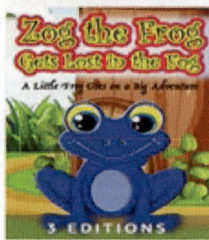 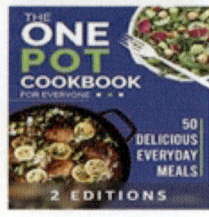

Hi! Check out more kids' books, coupons, specials and get in touch with Lucy at:

arrowtownpress.com